SHIPS OF THE SO[...]

PORTSMOUTH TO POOLE
by
Colin Hall

This book is a voyage through the Solent from East to West taking in all the ports and harbours open to commercial ships. We start at the Nab Tower on the approach to Portsmouth and finish in Swanage Bay just beyond Poole, by way of Southampton Water. We review all the different types of ships seen over a 25 year period roughly 1982 to 2004. From warships, tankers and cruise liners to ferries large and small, cross channel and cross river. We see preservation attempts successful and not so successful. In all a fascinating variety within a relatively short stretch of water.

This book is dedicated to my father for instilling in me a love of ships and the sea.

Colin Hall   July 2005

Front Cover. Still the queen of them all. The "Queen Elizabeth 2", or "QE2" as she is affectionately known, makes a majestic sight as she departs from Southampton on a cruise guided by a Red Funnel tug. Passengers on the Hythe Ferry have a fine view as she scurries pass towards the Town Quay.

20/7/98

Frontispiece. The sail training ship "Royalist" at anchor in Cowes Roads during the review of ships by the Queen celebrating the 50th anniversary of the D-day landings .
The ship silhouetted in the background is the US aircraft carrier "George Washington"

5/6/94

Back Cover. Evoking the heyday of paddle steamer excursions around the Solent. The "PS Waverley" comes alongside the pier at Bournemouth.

21/8/85

Colin Hall Publishing
Breamore
Hants
SP6 2DS

1. "Canberra". At full steam ahead heading east out of the Solent and about to pass the Nab Tower. Built by Harland & Wolff, Belfast, at 45,720 GRT in 1960 with steam turbines driving electric motors in what was then an unusual engines aft arrangement. Hence the funnels being above the stern. She remained a steam ship to the end.

5/6/94

2. "Vistafjord". Cunards cruise ship seen in the eastern Solent. Built in 1972 by Swan Hunter on Tyneside at 24,292 GRT for Den Norske Amerikalinje A/S of Oslo. Transfered to Norwegian American Cruises in 1980 she was purchased by Cunard three years later. Since this picture was taken she has been renamed "Caronia", a famous earlier Cunarder which had long links with Southampton.

5/6/94

3. "Duc de Normandie". Operated by Brittany Ferries, she heads out of the Solent on passage from Portsmouth to Caen. Built in 1978 in Heuseden, Holland as "Prinses Beatrix" for the Zeeland Steamship Company for their Hoek van Holland - Harwich service until 1986. This service was run in partnership with British Rail, later Sealink and finally taken over by Stena Line. She then moved to Portsmouth having been purchased by Brittany Ferries in 1985.

5/6/94

4. "C.S.Nevis". A cable laying ship operated by Cable & Wireless responsible for laying and repairing submarine communications cables at sea.

5/6/94

5. "H.M.S. Fearless" & "State of Maine". H.M.S. Fearless was built by Harland & Wolff of Belfast in 1965. She is an assault ship capable of launching landing craft from a submersible dock in the stern. She is of 12,500 GRT rising to 19,500 when her dock is flooded. "State of Maine" ,12,660 GRT, was built in 1951 as "President Hayes" for American President Lines of San Francisco by New York Shipbuilding of Camden NJ. However before final fitting out she was taken over by the US Navy and renamed "Upshur". In 1973 she was sold to the US Department of Commerce and renamed "State of Maine". Used as a training ship by Maine Maritime Academy. The two ships are seen together heading for France for the 50th D-day Anniversary celebrations.

5/6/94

6. "H.M.S. Ursula". An "Upholder" class of patrol submarine built in 1991 by Cammell Laird and powered by two 16 cylinder Paxman Valenta diesel engines. Made redundant by the changing role of the Royal Navy she was sold to the Canadian Navy in 2003 and renamed "Cornerbrook". Sister ship "HMS Upholder" was in the news when her transfer to Canada as the "Chicoutimi" was tragically eclipsed by a fire on board shortly after departing the UK which resulted in loss of life and her having to be towed back and extensively repaired.

5/6/94

7. "H.M.S. Hecla". Built at Yarrow, Tyneside in 1965 of 2,733 GRT. She was a survey vessel responsible for the gathering of data for upgrading admiralty charts.

5/6/94

8. "Jeremiah OíBrien". Built in 1943 by New England Shipbuilding Corp, South Portland, Maine,USA of 7,176 GRT. One of the last WW2 "Liberty" ships of which over 2,500 were built. These basic cargo ships were built cheaply and quickly by being highly stan-dardised, prefabricated and of all welded construction. This ship was saved in 1978 as the "National Liberty Ship Memorial" and is normally stationed in San Francisco.

5/6/94

9. "Tenacity". A AP1-88 hovercraft operated by Hovertravel on their Portsmouth - Ryde service. It operates between slipways adjacent to Clarence Pier and Ryde Pier. The service started in 1965 with two SRN6 craft. These were replaced by two APP1-88 in 1982. It is seen approaching the Ryde slipway.

18/9/88

10. "Our Lady Patricia". A 30m catamaran built by Incat of Hobart, Tasmania in 1986. Operates a passenger only service between Ryde Pier Head and Portsmouth Harbour rail stations linking the isolated Isle of Wight line with the national network. This follows a tradition set up by the LSWR and LBSCR rail companies in 1880 and continued in railway ownership until privatised a century later. Now operated by Wightlink.

30/3/94

11. "SS Shieldhal". Built in 1955 by Lobnitz & Co of Renfrew, Scotland she actually looks older than her years. A 1,753 GRT steamship with triple expansion engines of 1,600 HP she was built as a sludge (sewerage) carrier. After years operating out of the Clyde, she was bought by Southern Water and brought south to Southampton. Retired into preservation when dumping of sewerage at sea was made illegal. Based still in Southampton she does regular cruises out into the Solent.

14/9/96

12. "Jeremiah O'Brien". Another view of this Liberty Ship (see photo 8), seen passing one of the Spithead Napoleonic forts.

5/6/94

13. "St Catherine". Built at Leith, Scotland in 1983 for the then Sealink car ferry service between Portsmouth Broad Street and Fishbourne. Of 2,038 GRT she was the first of four similar 77m craft which replaced older, smaller vessels on this busy route. Seen at the Fishbourne terminal this service started in 1927 by the Southern Railway. Now privatised this is currently operated by Wightlink.

20/3/00

14. "St Cecilia". Built at Selby, Yorks in 1986 and of 2,968 GRT she is seen approaching the slipway at Fishborne.

20/3/00

15. "St Helen". Built in 1983 at Leith and of 2.983 GRT and seen entering Wootton Creek heading for Fishbourne.

20/3/00

16. "St Clare". Built at Gdansk, Poland in 2001 she is larger at 86m and 3,500 Grt than the other vessels on this route. She also differs in having a central bridge so is completely double ended saving having to reverse into the terminal at Portsmouth.

20/10/03

17. "Balmoral". Built in 1949 by J.I.Thornycroft at their yard in Woolston, Southampton (now sadly gone), she is a 688 GRT diesel ship with a long association with the Solent. Operated by Red Funnel between Southampton and Cowes until retirement in 1968 she was then sold to P & A Campbell for service in the Bristol Channel until 1980. After a spell in Dundee as a floating pub she was purchased by Waverley Steam Navigation, owners of the P S Waverley as a running mate. She still returns to the Solent for short programmes of cruises or special events.

5/6/94

18. "Pride of Winchester". Built at Aalborg, Denmark in 1975 as "Viking Viscount" for Townsend Thoresen on their Felixstowe to Zeebrugge service. Transferred to Portsmouth in 1985 and renamed "Pride of Winchester" following the takeover by P & O European Ferries. Withdrawn not long after this picture was taken and sold to Greek owners as "Vitsentzos Kornaros". Seen approaching the entrance to Portsmouth Harbour with Southsea and the Nelson Monument in the background.

5/6/94

19. "St Helen". Already seen in photo 15 now pictured heading out from Portsmouth into the Solent bound for Fishbourne.

5/6/94

20. "HMS Illustrious and HMY Britannia". "Illustrious" was built in 1982 by Swan - Hunter she is an aircraft carrier of 19,500 GRT with a deployment of 8 Sea-Harrier VTOL fighters and 10 Sea King helicopters. The "Britannia" was built on Clydeside at John Browns shipyard in 1954. Now a static museum ship in Leith, Scotland, she is seen here carrying the Queen to a review of ships in Spithead for the 50th anniversary of the D-day landings. "Illustrious" is acting as her escort.

5/6/94

21. "St Catherine". The Wightlink ferry already shown in 13, now seen entering Portsmouth Harbour from Fishbourne.

8/12/96

22. "St Faith". The final ship of the Saint quartet, built in 1990 at Selby, Yorkshire, and seen passing through the harbour entrance at Portsmouth with the submarine base at Gosport in the background.

8/12/96

23. "Southsea". The first of three post war ferries built for the Southern Railway in 1948 by Wm Denny of Dumbarton, Scotland. Of 986GRT and powered by twin Sulzer 8 cylinder diesels she served on the Portsmouth to Ryde IOW run until replaced by the catamarans in 1986. She remained in in service as reserve vessel and on Solent cruises until finally withdrawn and laid up. She has since led a nomadic existence following a series of failed preservation attempts. Seen here entering Portsmouth Harbour at the end of a cruise.

29/8/88

24 "Normandie". Built at Turku, Finland for Britanny Ferries and their Portsmouth to Caen route. She is seen passing Gunwharf Quay.

14/9/96

25. "Pride of Cherbourg". Built at Aarlborg, Denmark for Townsend Thoresen in 1975 as "Viking Valiant" for their Southampton to Le Havre route. This was transferred to Portsmouth in 1984. Rebuilt in 1986 with extended length and number of decks increasing GRT from 9,735 to 14,760. In 1989 she was renamed "Pride of Le Havre" following the takeover by P&O. Transferred to the Cherbourg run in 1994 and renamed "Pride of Cherbourg". Replaced 2002.

19/3/01

26. "Pride of Le Havre". Of 33,336 GRT she was built at Bremerhaven, Germany in 1989 as "Olau Hollandia" for TT Lines but operated by Olau on their Sheerness - Vlissingen run. Following the collapse of this service in 1994, she was taken on by P&O to provide greater capacity on their Portsmouth - Le Havre run.

19/3/01

27. "St Cecilia". First seen in 14 at Fishbourne, now pictured at the Broad Street terminal of Wightlink in Old Portsmouth.

10/8/97

28. "Brading". She was the second of the three post war Denny ships for the Southern Railwayís IOW service to Ryde. Seen here laid up alongside the servicing pontoon off Portsmouth Harbour station soon after the entry into service of the first catamarans.

9/6/86

29. "Gosport Queen". Built 1966 of 159GRT she operates the frequent short ferry link between Portsmouth Harbour railway station and Gosport town centre.

19/3/01

30. "Portsmouth Queen" and "Pride of Gosport". Two generations of Gosport ferry seen together. "Portsmouth Queen" built in 1966 of 159GRT, length 30.5m and carries 250 passengers whilst the "Pride of Gosport" was built in 2001 of 250GRT, length 32.6m and carries 300 passengers.

31/3/03

31. "Mont St Michel". Built at Krimpen ann den Ijssel, Rotterdam in 2002 for the Portsmouth to Caen route of Britanny Ferries. 35,592GRT.

27/3/04

32. "Pride of Portsmouth". The former "Olau Britannia" from the short lived Sheerness to Vlissingen route shows off the then new P&O corporate colours. Compare with her sister in picture 26. She is seen arriving from Le Harve.

31/3/03

33 & 34. "HMS Victory". Built in 1765 by Chatham Dockyard, Kent as a "ship of the line", the frontline in naval war power. Led a very active service culminating in the Battle of Tragalgar in 1805. Lord Nelson died on board during that engagement. From 1812 she was in stationary use in Portsmouth Harbour until 1922 when her deteriation led to being docked in No 2 graving dock where she has remained ever since. Now permanently confined to her dry dock and cosmetically restored she is still in commission with the Royal Navy and is open to the public daily under guided tours by serving seamen.

8/12/96

35. "HMS Warrior". Built in 1860 by the Thames Ironworks & Shipbuilding Company of Blackwell, London she was the first warship built of iron at 9,210GRT with screw propulsion powered by a 1250hp steam engine. She never fired a shot in anger. From 1881 she was used as a training vessel until 1929 when she became a landing stage for fuel at Pembroke. In 1979 taken to Hartlepool for restoration. Now displayed alongside Portsmouth Harbour railway station and open to the public.

36. "Holland One". First submarine built for the Royal Navy. Built in 1901 by Vickers at Barrow where submarines are still built for the Royal Navy today. Constructed of steel at 105GRT with a length of 19.35m she was powered by gasoline and electric motors. Designed by John Holland after whom she is named. She sank off Plymouth not long after entering service but was raised in the early 1980's and restored. Now on display at the Submarine Museum, Gosport.

37. "Midget Submarine". World War Two mini submarine on display at the Submarine Museum.

38. "HMS Alliance". Built in 1945 by Vickers Armstrong, Barrow and powered by diesel and electric motors. She is 85.85m long and of 1120GRT.

39. "Bustler". Royal Navy harbour tug of 375GRT built in 1981 by R. Dunstons.

19/3/01

40. "RFA Brambleleaf" and "Setter". Seen alongside the Royal Fleet Auxillary depot at Gosport. "Brambleleaf" was built in 1980 by Cammell Laird at 37,747GRT and a length of 170m. The "Setter" is a 152GRT, 29m dog class tug of a batch supplied in the late 1960's.

41. "USS Mount Witney". Built in 1971 at Newport News shipyard she is a 7,234grt Amphibious Command Ship of the US navy. She is seen in Portmouth Harbour on a courtesy visit. Used as fleet flagships this class of vessel provides accommodation for Navy amphibious task force commanders, Marine assault force commanders and their staffs.

14/9/96

42. "HMS Invincible". Built in 1979 by Vickers at Barrow she was the first of three new aircraft carriers for the Royal Navy designed for the then new VTOL Harrier jet aircraft .

31/3/03

43 & 44. "PS Ryde". Built in 1937 by William Denny of Dumbarton, Scotland for the Southern Railway and was their last paddle steamer. She served connecting passengers arriving on trains at Portsmouth Harbour with Ryde Pier and the isolated rail network on the Isle of Wight. A job now undertaken by high speed catamarans. She remained in service until 1969 and eventually ended up in a mud berth on the River Medina halfway between Cowes and Newport. Used variously as nightclub, restaurant and marina offices she is currently derelict. There have been several attempts to save her but so far they have all failed. Lets hope someone will succeed and the "Ryde" will be seen again on the solent running in partnership with the "Southsea".

20/10/03

45. "No5" Chain ferry linking East and West Cowes across the medina river. Built at East Cowes in 1976 for the Isle of Wight council who run her. This ferry is free for passengers but cars have to pay.

11/10/02

46. "Bergen Castle" & "Sunk". "Bergen Castle" is on charter to Red Funnel Ferries whilst each of their three "Raptor" class car ferries goes to Gdansk in Poland for enlarging. The lightship is at the Trinity House depot. The "Sunk" lightship station is in the North Sea east of Norwich.

29/03/04

47. "MTB Bladerunner Two". Built in 2003 this is a 110GRT motor barge designed to carry blades for wind turbines from a factory in Cowes to Southampton Docks.

29/03/04

48. "Split Two". One of the numerous dredgers that ply the Solent and its various small quays. This one is based at Poole and is seen entering the River Medina at Cowes on its way to a gravel quay near Newport.

11/10/03

49. "Red Falcon". One of the trio of "Raptor" class car ferries used by Red Funnel on their hourly link between Southampton and East Cowes. Built at Port Glasgow for this service in 1994 replacing an ageing fleet of smaller, locally built ships.

11/10/03

50. "Red Eagle". The third of the "Raptor" class ferries she was built at Port Glasgow in 1996 at 3028GRT. These ships have now been rebuilt with a central T-section inserted giving them an extra car deck and longer length.

11/10/03

51. "Red Jet 3". Built in 1998 by FBM Marine of Cowes of 213GRT and 32.9m in length she was the last of three locally built high speed catamarans replacing the "Sheerwater" hydrofoils which dated from the late 70's and earlier 80's. These craft are used on the half hourly passenger only link between Southampton and West Cowes.

11/10/03

52. "Red Jet 4". Red Funnel went to Australia for their fourth catamaran. Built in 2003 by North West Bay Ships of Hobart, Tasmania she is of 345GRT and a length of 39m.

11/10/03

53. "TS Royalist". Enters Cowes under light sail.

20/10/03

54. "N1387". Preserved WW2 RAF rescue launch seen in the Solent off Cowes during the celebrations for the 50th anniversary of the D-day landings. Many of these vessels were built in boatyards in Cowes and Southampton.

5/6/94

55. "Canberra" anchored in Cowes Roads prior to be reviewed by H M The Queen during the 50 years D-Day anniversary.

5/6/94

56. "Vistafjord" also anchored in Cowes Roads on the same occasion.

5/6/94

57. "USS Guam" anchored in Cowes Roads for the 50th D-Day celebrations. Built in Philadelphia in 1965 for the US navy she is a "Iwo Jima" class amphibious assault ship. Of 10,722 GRT she can carry a full Marine battalion complete with helicopter support.

5/6/94

58. "USS George Washington" is a "Nimitz" class aircraft carrier of the US navy. Built on a massive scale and nuclear powered she is a formidable force carrying up to ten squadrons of different attack and surveillance aircraft. She took ten years to complete from ordering in 1982 to commissioning in 1992 in Norfolk, Virginia by Newport News Shipbuilding. She was over here for the D-Day celebrations.

5/6/94

59. "Uko Bluefin", a suction dredger enters Southampton Water off Calshot.

29/3/04

60. "Saga Pearl" the 12,331GRT cruise ship operated by Saga Holidays and formerly the Swan Hellenic "Minivera", turns into Southampton Water from the Solent returning from a cruise.

11/10/03

61. "Mupa Wonsild", a 1,780GRT chemical tanker anchored off Fawley awaiting a load. Empty tankers are a common sight anchored around the Solent after delivering to Fawley Refinery and awaiting their next assignment. Built in 1974 as the "Benvenue" being renamed in 1989 by her then new owners.

14/9/96

62. "Danchem West" a 1,666GRT chemical tanker built in 1992 is seen anchored of Fawley.

14/9/96

63. "Agean Breeze" sails up Southampton Water with a cargo of imported cars. The import and export of cars through Southampton is now a massive business with ships to match.

11/10/03

64. "Donald Bedford", built in 1981 of 681GRT is a common sight in Southampton Water. One of many locally based dredgers that extract sands and gravels from off the Isle of Wight to wharves on the Rivers Itchen and Test in Southampton. She achieved notoriety locally when she demolished part of the Hythe Pier in 2002 whilst her skipper was under the influence of alcohol. Luckily the pier was soon repaired.

11/10/03

65. "Dart 8". Built in 1980 as "Xi Feng Kou" at Sakaide in Japan for China Ocean Shipping Co. Taken over by Dart Line in 1999 and renamed for their Dartford - Zeebrugge service. She is a 22,748GRT RoRo vessel which was operating under charter to the Ministry of Defence sailing out of Marchwood when seen across the salt marsh at Ashlett Creek, near Fawley.

31/8/03

66. "Oriana". Seen passing Ashlett Creek this 1995 built 69,153grt cruise ship is seen outward bound from Southampton heading for the Mediterranean.

31/8/03

67. "Victoria" Built in 1965 by John Brown Shipbuilders of Clydebank at 26,678GRT as "Kungsholm" for Swedish America Line of Gothenbourg. Sold to P&O in 1978 becoming their "Sea Princess" before being renamed again as "Victoria" in 1995. In 2003 she was sold to Kyma Ship Management for charter to Holiday Kreuzfahrten of Germany and again renamed as "Mona Lisa". Seen off Fawley from the top deck of a Red Funnel Ferry which has just overtaken her.

6/8/99

68. "Bro Jupiter". A liquid petroleum gas tanker seen alongside the terminal at Fawley refinery.

29/3/04

69. "Ievoli Speed" one of many different chemical tankers to be seen at Fawley.

29/3/04

70. "Bro Sincero". A 11,855grt tanker built in 2002 for Brostrom Van Ommeren Shipping of Sweden.

11/10/03

71. "Kuban". A Russian tanker of 88,692GRT built in 1976 and seen at Fawley.

29/3/04

72. "Esso Fawley". Built in 1967 of 10,631GRT she is a small oil tanker for distribution of petrolium products to coastal depots from its base at Fawley refinery.

5/6/94

73. "Cowes Castle". Built in 1965 by J.I.Thorneycroft of Woolston, Southampton for local use between Southampton and East Cowes for Red Funnel Ferries. As built she was 191ft in length and of 786Grt but in 1975 she was extended to 221ft and 912GRT. This work converted her to a drive through ship. In 1994 she was sold to Jadrolinija, a Croatian ferry operator becoming the "Nehaj" after being replaced by the first of the "Raptors".

29/5/91

74. "Shearwater 3". A Hydrofoil of type RHS70 built in 1972 by Cantiere Navale Rodriguez of Messina, Italy. Of 62GRT and powered by a Maybach Mercedes Benz 1,350hp V12 diesel it was capable of 32 knots. Used on the Southampton to West Cowes passenger only service she was replaced shortly after this picture was taken by the first of the Red Jet catamarans.

29/5/91

75. "Norris Castle". Built in 1968 she is sister ship to "Cowes Castle" and shares a similar history right down to being sold to the same Croatian ferry company on her retirement from service on Southampton Water. She became the "Lourjenac".

30/4/93

76. "Netley Castle". Built in 1974 of 1,183GRT at Ryton Marine, Wallsend on Tyne. She was the first Red Funnel ship not to be built locally and was the first double ended ferry on the route. In 1997 she was also sold to Jadrolinija and renamed "Sis".

30/4/93

77. "BBC Anglia". Seen anchored off Hythe offloading military containers into landing craft for transfer to Marchwood. The war in Iraq saw the charter of many merchant ships to the "Ministry of Defence".

29/3/04

78. "Queen Elizabeth 2". Harking back to an earlier conflict she is seen on her triumphal return from the "Falkland Islands". Built in 1967 by Upper Clyde Shipbuilders at 65,863grt as a steam turbine ship. She was later to be converted to diesel. Cunard tradition was broken by having a black and white funnel but the more traditional colours were used later.

1982

79. "Canberra". Seen arriving in Southampton out of the early morning mist at the end of her final cruise. Always a popular ship, which also served in the Falklands war, a large armada of small boats escorts her into Southampton for the last time.

30/9/97

80. "Queen Mary 2". Built in 2003 at St Nazaire in France at 148,528grt, she is seen arriving in Southampton for the very first time. Despite the extremely foggy morning a large flotilla of small pleasure craft braved the conditions to escort her in.

26/12/03

81. "Kaga". Built in 1988 for Nippon Yusen Kaisha (NYK Line) she is a 51,047grt container ship and is seen arriving in Southampton from the far east. The tug with a line already attached for the tricky turning manoeuvre on reaching the container terminal is "Hamtun". She was built for Red Funnel in 1985 by McTay Marine of Bromborough for towage duties at Southampton and is of 250grt.

29/5/91

82. "Flying Kestrel". This tug is actually part of the ensemble in picture 81. She is travelling backwards and the line you can see is attached to the stern of the "Kaga". The tug is acting as a "brake" to slow the container ship down and to be ready to swing the large ship round into her berth. She was one of two 243grt German built vessels built in 1976 and purchased by Alexander Towing in 1986 for use at Southampton.

29/5/91

83. "Welsh Bay". She is a suction dredger operated by Associated British Ports, owners of Southampton Docks, for keeping the river channels open to the large ships that use the port. Built in 1971 she is of 2,837grt.

29/5/91

84. "Sir Winston Churchill". One of the many sail training ships that regularly visit Southampton. Travelling under power with sails stored she is about to be overtaken by one of the Red Funnel "Raptor" car ferries.

8/6/95

85. "SS Shieldhall". Seen here moored in the Ocean Village, her Southampton home for many years following her arrival from Glasgow. She is now kept elsewhere in the docks, usually 48 berth.

30/4/93

86. "Arco Dart". Built in 1990 she is a 1,309 grt dredger operated by Hanson Aggregates Marine Ltd based at Burnley Wharf on Southampton's River Itchen and seen from the bridge over that river. In the left background can be seen the 1990 built "Sand Harrier" of 3,751grt and operated by Ready Mixed Concrete from Baltic Wharf. Also on view are some exUS navy tugs which have been refurbished by a yard on the Itchen for further private use after many years mothballed at a navy depot at Hythe.

25/10/03

87. "Donald Redford". A dredger operated by Northwood (Fareham) Ltd and seen unloading on a wharf at Woolston in the shadow of the Itchen Bridge. This ship was seen underway in picture 64. A week after this picture was taken she was involved in the colli-sion with Hythe Pier when she overshot the turn out of the River Itchen into Southampton Water. Her captain was drunk at the time.

25/10/03

88. "Hexham Lass". Further up the River Itchen by Northam Bridge this old dredger was photographed at a wharf used at various times for timber, aggregates and scrap metal.

1985

89. "Southsea". More recently this wharf was the last home of this local veteran. See picture 23. Sadly this preservation attempt failed and she was reportedly being scrapped as this book went to press.

25/10/03

90. "APL Cyprine". Neptune Orient Lines of Singapore operate this 1997 built 65,465grt container ship seen passing the end of Hythe Pier on a winters afternoon.

12/01/04

91. "Baltic Breeze". Built in 1983 at 10,881grt she is a vehicle carrier operated by Wallenius Lines. She is used on the growing export / import trade in cars between Southampton and the far east.

20/7/03

92. "Dora Baltea". Another bulk car carrier this time operated by Grimaldi Lines.

20/7/98

93. "Black Prince". Built in 1966 at 9,499grt by Lubecker Flendwerke AG, Lubeck, Germany for Fred Olsen Oslo and DET Bergenske D/S Kristiansand, Norway. Registered as "Black Prince" but operated then as "Venus" in the summer months Kristiansand - Amsterdam - Harwich then using her registered name in the winter on cruises, originally to the Canary Islands from London. Taken over solely by Fred Olsen in 1986 and converted for full time cruising including removal of car decks.

31/8/03

94. "Queen Elizabeth 2". Compare with picture 78. She has now been converted to diesel electric propulsion. The work being carried out at Lloyd Werft Bremerhaven in 1986. At the same time her new funnel was painted in the traditional Cunard colours. She is seen departing Southampton escorted by the tug "Hamtun".

20/7/98

95. "Caronia". The former cruise ship "Vistafjord" seen earlier in pictures 2 & 56 now resplendent in full traditional Cunard colours. She has taken the name of a Cunarder of an earlier generation which had a long and cherished association with Southampton. She has since been sold to Saga Holidays.

20/7/03

96. "Queen Mary 2". Seen earlier in picture 80 we now see her prior to sailing to Fort Lauderdale USA on her maiden voyage. She had spent three weeks in Southampton following her delivery voyage from France for final fitting out and short shake down trips round the Isle of Wight and to the Channel Islands. Alongside are two local car ferries "Red Eagle" and "St Clare" being used as chartered grandstand platforms to watch her departure. Normally the paths of these two ferries do not cross being used on parallel routes from the mainland to the Isle of Wight so this is a very rare sight.

12/1/04

97. "Queen Mary 2". All lit up and ready to go. From her berth she was towed backwards by tugs until she was alongside Mayflower Park. From there a spectacular firework display gave her a grand send off before she made her way down Southampton Water.

12/1/04

98. "Victoria". Seen earlier in picture 67. Shown here leaving Southampton on one of her last season cruises with P&O. Renamed "Mona Lisa" by new owners.

2/6/02

99. "Aurora". One of the new generation of cruise liners with P&O. Built in 2000 of 76,152grt.

2/6/02

100. "Norway". Built by Chantiers de l'Atlantique, St Nazaire, France as the "France" in 1960 for French Line / Cie Generale Transatlantique. She was used on liner services from Le Havre to New York via Southampton. After trans-Atlantic services finished she was used for cruising but by 1974 these had become uneconomic and she was laid up in Le Havre. Sold to Lauritz Kloster, Oslo in 1979 who extensively refit her including replacing her steam turbines with diesel engines and renamed her "Norway". Transferred to Norwegian Caribbean Lines in 1984 and spent most of her time cruising out of east coast US ports. A frequent visitor as "France" her visits became rare as "Norway". Seen here departing after a refit in Southampton.

20/7/98

101. "Norway". Another view of this beautiful ship this time departing on a cruise.

30/8/97

102. "Mermaid". Built in 1987 at 2,820grt for the Trinity House lighthouse service. Used in conjunction with maintenance work with navigation buoys, lightships and lighthouses. The storage area for buoys can be seen ahead of the bridge with its derricks for placing and retrieving them at sea.

29/5/91

103. "Kristina Regina". Operated by Kristina Cruises of Finland she is an unusual ship and a rare visitor to Southampton. Built in 1960 and of 4,295grt she was originally named "Bore" changing to "Borea" in 1977 and receiving her current name in 1987.

5/6/94

104. "Norway". Another view of this fine ship this time berthed at the QE2 terminal.

30/8/97

105. "Asian Explorer". One of the super car carriers operated by Eukor Car Carriers Inc of South Korea. These huge floating boxes are an increasingly common sight in Southampton some distinguishable by the differing colour schemes of their operators. They have little in the way of fine lines especially the larger ones.

20/7/03

106. "Calshot" & "Hual Oceana". "Calshot" was built by J I Thorneycroft of Woolston, Southampton in 1930 for Red Funnel as a tug tender. This meant she was fitted with passenger accommodation to go down to Cowes Roads to pick up passengers from liners which did not need to call at Southampton. Sold to Ireland in 1964 for use as a ferry in Galway. Now back in Southampton in an attempt to restore her. As Southampton's last link with the era of great passenger liners she is of immense historic importance to both the port and the city. Despite this little money can be found to restore her and it will be tragic if the preservation attempt fails. She is seen dewarfed by "Hual Oceana" a 58,947grt car carrier built in 2003 operated by Hual AS of Norway.

20/7/03

107. "Fidelio" & "Brightwell". The 47,219grt Wallenius Wilhelmsen bulk car carrier "Fidelio" built in 1987 is seen berthing at Southampton's Eastern Dock with the Red Funnel tug "Brightwell" standing by. The "Brightwell" is a 256grt tug built in 1986.

21/9/94

108. "P S Waverley". The paddle steamer "Waverley" was built in 1946 by A & J Inglis of Glasgow for the London & North Eastern Railway to replace a paddle steamer of the same name lost at Dunkirk. She was employed as a pleasure steamer and ferry around the Clyde, its outlying islands and sea lochs. She is the last sea going paddle steamer in the world.. Retired by Caledonian Macbrayne Ltd in 1973 and sold to the Paddle Steamer Preservation Society for £1. Following two years restoration she returned to service and now operates almost throughout the year. Visiting many parts of the country under the management of the Waverley Steam Navigation Company she normally operates an extensive programme of excursions throughout the area covered by this book for four weeks every September. She also appears for special events such as here when she was in Southampton to greet the "Canberra" at the end of her last cruise.

30/9/97

109. "Dar Pomorza". Built in 1909 by Blohm & Voss, Hamburg for the German Schoolship Association as a fully rigged sail training vessel. Bought by Poland in 1929 after spending a few years out of use and returned to service. Retired in 1981 but subsequently returned to service and regularly to be seen at "Tall Ship" events.

14/4/00

110. "Kruzenshtern". Built in 1926 by JC Tecklenborg, Wesermunde, Germany as the Padua as a four mast cargo barque. Of 3545grt and length 97.38m she was now used as a sail training ship in Russia from the end of the second world war. Now sails under the Estonian flag and based in Talinn.

14/4/00

111. "Sedov". Built in 1921 by Germania Werft, Kiel, Germany as a four mast sailing barque. Served as a cargo vessel until the end of WW2 when transferred to Russia as a sail training ship. She is still owned by the Russian government.

14/4/00

112. "Candi". Built 1971 by Dubigeon-Normandie SA, Nantes, France as "Massalia" for Nouvelle Cie de Paquebots, Marseilles for use as a car ferry between Marseilles and the Canary Islands via Casablanca. In 1983 purchased by Stena Cargo Line of Stockholm as "Stena Baltica" but in the following year sent to Mexico for day cruises as "Island Fiesta" until damaged by an engine room fire in 1988. Renamed "Scandinavian Star" and returned to Europe in 1990 for service on the Frederikshavn to Oslo run chartered by Danish Da-No Line. A month after entering service on this run she again caught fire resulting in the loss of 158 lives and being declared a total loss. Towed first to Copenhagen then Hull where she was renamed "Candi" and finally Southampton where she was laid up for many years.

29/5/91

113. "Brightwell". A 256grt tug built in 1986 for the Alexandra Towing Company at Great Yarmouth for use at the port of Felixstowe before being transferred to Southampton. Now under the management of Adsteam following the merger of the Red Funnel and Alexadra tug fleets. She is seen here passing the Town Quay.

21/9/94

114. "Flying Osprey" & "Aya II". The tug "Flying Osprey" is sister ship to "Flying Kestrel" seen in picture 82. The "Aya II" is a 11,947grt bulk car carrier built in 1978 as "Pioneer Ace". Renamed in 1989 and operated by Linea Mexicana.

21/9/94

115. "Liverpool Bay". Built for P & O Containers Ltd in 1972 at 56,822grt and is seen passing Town Quay.

8/6/95

116. "Arco Severn". Built in 1973 this 1,599grt suction dredger was operated by ARC Marine Ltd but was laid up near the Town Quay when photographed.

20/7/03

117. "Hotspur IV". Built in 1946 at the Rowhedge Ironworks, Colchester for service between Hythe Pier and Southampton Town Quay. She is shown in her original blue colours.

29/5/91

118. "Hotspur IV". Following the take over of the Hythe ferry service by White Horse Ferries the livery was changed to red and white. This wonderful old vessel was still plying the route at the time of writing but is very much the reserve ship.

21/9/94

119. "Bergen Castle" & "Red Jet 1". "Bergen Castle" was purchased by Red Funnel in 2003 so that each of the Raptor class car ferries could be withdrawn in turn for enlargement in Poland. She was built at Lolan, Norway in 1976 for service around Bergen as the "Nordhordland" and is of 1220grt. "Red Jet 1" was the first of the high speed catamarans for the passenger only Southampton Town Quay to West Cowes service which phased out the hydrofoils. Built in 1991 by FBM Marine of Cowes she has not strayed far.

11/10/03

120. "Red Osprey". The first Raptor class ferry to be rebuilt seen shortly after her return to service. She has been heightened to accommodate an upper car deck and lengthened. This increased their length from 83.6m to 93.2m and registered tonnage from 3028grt to 3953grt. The work was carried out at Gdansk by the same shipyard that built Wightlink's "St Clare". The new work can be clearly seen above the original open deck forward of the superstructure which was also increased in height by 3m.

29/3/04

121. "L4001 Ardennes". Built in 1977 by Brooke Marine this vessel is an army landing craft of 1,050grt designed to carry up to five Chieftain tanks or other payload up to 350tons. She has bow doors for discharging load or troops directly onto beaches. Seen here departing from the military port at Marchwood which is located on the opposite side of Southampton water to the Western Docks and upriver from Hythe.

5/6/94

122. "Sea Crusader". Built 1996 as the "Celestine" for Cobelfret Ferries in Sakaide, Japan, but almost immediately taken up for charter by the Ministry of Defence. She returned to Cobelfret in 2003 for use on their Zeebrugge - Immingham service, is of 23,986grt and is one of six sisterships in that fleet.

21/8/02

123. "Pavels Parenago" & "Acritas". Two ships shown in Southampton Western Docks of which I can find nothing. The nearest was a refrigerated vessel possibly unloading bananas because it is along side the Geest terminal before that was relocated to Portsmouth Harbour. I would be pleased to hear from anyone with information on these ships so that I can update future editions.

8/6/95

124. "Genoa" & "Sundream". The P&O / Nedlloyd container ship "Genoa" is seen leaving Southampton and passes the Mytravel cruise ship "Sundream". The "Genoa" was built in 1998 and is of 31,333grt. The 22,945grt "Sundream" was launched in 1969 at the Wartsila yard, Helsinki as the "Song of Norway" for Royal Caribbean Cruise Line operating out of Miami. Renamed "Sundream" in 1997 and operated by Sun Cruises for Mytravel out of Southampton.

31/8/03

125. "Norway". The former French Line flagship "France" is seen in the King George V dry dock at the head of Southampton Water. She is undergoing a refit which is the reason for this visit.

18/9/96

126. "Caedmon". Departs Lymington for Yarmouth on the half hourly link to the Isle of Wight. Built in Dundee in 1973 of 764grt, initially for the Portsmouth Harbour (Broad Street) to Fishbourne service operated by British Rail, then transferred to their Lymington base in 1983 where she joined her two sister ships. The railway reached Lymington via a branch from Brockenhurst in 1860 but a service to the IOW was already well established and steamships had been running since 1830. The London & South Western Railway then took over the service running from the pier station at Lymington with connections to and from trains which continues today. The railway has always seen this route as very secondary to its Portsmouth - IOW operations including the passing down of ships. It was the development of car ferries which brought this service to prominence. Formed into Sealink for privatisation and sold to the American company Sea Containers alongside the rest of British Rail's shipping division. In 1990 the IOW services were reformed into Wightlink whilst the rest of Sealink was sold to Stena Lines. The company was bought out by its management in 2001.

30/9/97

127. "Cenred" & "Cenwolf". These are the other two vessels on the Lymington to Yarmouth run. Built also Dundee in 1973 they are of a slightly lower 761grt. All three ships can carry up to 512 passengers and 58 cars. They are seen berthed at the Lymington terminal.

30/9/97

128. "Caedmon". The approach to Lymington in very attractive as is the crossing as a whole. The salt marshes at the mouth of the Lymington River with views of the Needles and Hurst Point lighthouses, close in to be replaced by numerous boat marinas, moorings and yards. It is with great skill these ships are brought through these waters as they run a gauntlet of small boats darting across their path.

30/9/97

129. "Cenred". Passing one of the many small boat marinas in Lymington.

30/9/97

130. "Cenwolf". Seen in mid passage to Yarmouth. The three boat service means that ships pass at the mouth of the river and off Yarmouth as seen here.

11/9/99

131. "Cenred". Approaching the terminal at Yarmouth seen from the vantage point of the old Victorian pier.

11/9/99

132. "Caedmon". Approaching the link span at Yarmouth.

133. "RNLI Joy & John Wade". On station at Yarmouth a Tyne class lifeboat in the small boat harbour.

134. "PS Waverley". The paddle steamer "Waverley" comes alongside the pier at Bournemouth. She visits the south coast regularly with an extensive programme of cruises with three weeks usually spent in the Solent.

21/8/85

135. "PS Waverley". Evoking memories of the heyday of paddle steamer services round the Solent and along the Dorset coast the "Waverley" backs away from the pier at Bournemouth on an evening cruise.

21/8/85

136. "Sand Swift". A dredger operated by RMC Marine heading out to sea from Poole Harbour having just passed through the narrows at Sandbanks. On of many similar ships operating from the Solents ports not just for keeping those ports clear for navigation but the commercial exploitation of sand and gravel beds off the Isle of Wight.

25/9/97

137. "PS Waverley" & "Condor Express". Ferries of two distinct eras meet off Shell Bay at the entrance to Poole Harbour. The "Waverley" is outward bound on a Dorset coast cruise whilst the Seacat "Condor Express" operated by Condor Ferries arrives from the Channel Islands. She is an 86m Incat catamaran built Hobart, Australia in 1996.

6/9/99

138. "Barfleur". Seen approaching the entrance to Poole Harbour she was, at this time, operated by Brittany Ferries subsidiary Truckline sailing between Cherbourg and Poole. Built in Helsinki in 1992 especially for this route, which it has made its own, with up to three crossings a day and a high standard of service on an all year round basis. She is of 20,133grt and a length of 158m carrying up to 1212 passengers, 590 cars or 112 lorry trailers.

25/9/97

139. "Coutrances". Running alongside the "Barfleur" is the "Coutrances" which is freight only. Built in Le Havre in 1978 for Truckline to then upgrade this route in harness with a sister ship "Purbeck". The sister has moved on but "Coutrance" continues but at the time of writing a replacement is being discussed. She was lengthened to 125.2m and 6,507grt in 1986 increasing her capacity by a third to 58 road trailers.

11/6/00

140. "PS Waverley". Another view of the "Waverley" this time passing through the narrow entrance to Poole Harbour with the resort of Sandbanks in the background. To the left is the "Sandbanks Ferry" which plies its way back and forth across the harbour entrance on chains. This ferry is unusual in that it not only carries the usual foot passengers and small vehicles but also the Bournemouth to Swanage bus service.

21/8/85

141. "Bramble Bush Bay". The latest chain ferry on the Sandbanks run replacing the one in the previous picture in 1993. She was built at Hessle, on Humberside, and at 74.4m carries up to 48 cars.

20/9/00

142. "Union Moon". The Sandbanks ferry waits for this 1543grt 1985 built coaster to pass through the harbour entrance. She is a general cargo coaster operated by Union Transport Group.

22/7/02

143. "Condor Vitesse". A Condor Ferries Seacat turns to follow the deep water channel into Poole Harbour just after passing through the entrance. The landing stage in the right foreground is for the Brownsea Island ferry, the island itself is the wooded area directly behind.

11/9/02

144. "Barfleur". Outward bound for Cherbourg she sails from Poole turning into the narrow harbour entrance. Brownsea Island is in the left background. She now sports full Brittany Ferries livery having been repainted in 1999. Compare with picture 139.

11/9/02

145. "Whitchallenger". This is a 2002 built, Isle of Man registered, 2958grt tanker seen on the head of Poole docks. She is a frequent sighting around the Solent and is often to be seen in Southampton providing fuel for the large cruise liners. In the foreground is Poole Marina.

22/3/04

146. "Hebridean Spirit". Poole sometimes sees small cruise ships. Seen here is "Hebridean Spirit" operated by Hebridean Island Cruises berthed opposite the Town Quay. This 4,200grt ship was built in 1991 as "Renaissance Six" and carried three other names before assuming the guise seen here in 2001. She is small enough to go almost anywhere.

11/9/02

147. "Lia-C". A 2001 built 2,999grt general cargo vessel operated by Carisbrooke Shipping. An increasing number of these small ships are now using Poole making it a busy little port which has the advantage of both road and rail access.

22/3/04

148. "Union Jack". A Georgetown registered cargo ship unloads opposite the Town Quay at Poole.

22/3/04

149. "Coutrances". Another view of Brittany Ferries freight vessel operating under the Truckline banner, this time at her berth and seen from the deck of the "Barfleur".

11/6/00

150. "PS Waverley". This paddle steamer visits every year and is seen laid up for the night on Poole Town Quay.

151. "Herbert Ballam". This tug is operated by the Poole Harbour Commissioners and is seen at its base on the Town Quay. Built in 1998 she is of 63grt and has a bollard pull of 19 tonnes.

22/3/04

152. "Brownsey Island Ferries". These distinctive yellow liveried vessels are seen moored at their operating base on the quay whilst laid up for the winter.

22/3/04

153. "Bournemouth Belle". The other local ferry company operating out of Poole are Dorset Belle Cruises. They connect Swanage, Bournemouth and Poole using three similar vessels. "Bournemouth Belle" is seen calling at Brownsea Island astern of a departing Brownsea Island Ferry.

11/9/02

154. "SS Shieldhall". Just south west of Poole Harbour is Swanage Bay. In the summer months occasional visits are made by preserved ships on cruises along the Dorset coast or in connection with visits to the steam railway at Swanage. The "SS Shieldhall" is seen on a non landing visit. The recently restored Victorian pier is used for landing passengers which is also used by the regular services of the Dorset Belle ferries to Bournemouth and Poole.

31/7/99